ROMEO AND JULIET

Opera in Five Acts

Libretto by

J. BARBIER and M. CARRÉ

Music by

CHARLES GOUNOD

The English Version by
DR. THEO. BAKER

With an Essay on the
Story of the Opera by

W. J. HENDERSON

Ed. 454

G. SCHIRMER, Inc.

DISTRIBUTED BY

HAL•LEONARD
CORPORATION
7777 W. BLUEMOUND RD. P.O. BOX 13819 MILWAUKEE, WI 53213

Romeo and Juliet.

First performed at the Théâtre Lyrique, Paris, April 27, 1867.

Characters of the Drama,

With the Original Cast as presented at the first Performance.

JULIET	Soprano		Mme. CARVALHO
STEPHANO	Soprano		Mme. DARAM
GERTRUDE	Mezzo-soprano		Mme. DUCLOS
ROMEO	Tenor		M. MICHOT
TYBALT	Tenor		M. PUGET
BENVOLIO	Tenor		M. LAURENT
MERCU IO	Baritone		M. BARRÉ
PARIS	Baritone		M. LAVEISSIÈRE
GREGORIO	Baritone		M. TROY (jeune)
CAPULET	Basso cantante		M TROY
FRIAR LAURENCE	Bass		M. CAZAUX
THE DUKE	Bass		M. CHRISTOPHE

Guests of the Capulets; Relatives and Retainers of
the Capulets and Montagues.

SCENE, VERONA.

Act I.—Capulet's Palace.   Act II.—The Garden of Juliet.   Act III.—The Cell
of Friar Laurence ; then a Public Square before Capulet's Palace.
Act IV.—Juliet's Chamber.   Act V.—Tomb of the Capulets.

" Romeo and Juliet."

Charles Gounod was born in Paris, June 17, 1818, and died in that city, October
18, 1893. His "Roméo et Juliette" occupies the second position of merit on the
brief list of his operas, the first place, of course, being awarded to "Faust". The
excellence of the libretto of the latter opera naturally led Gounod to go to its makers,
when he conceived the desire to write a lyric work on the familiar love-tragedy of
Shakespeare. That he should have entertained such an idea was almost inevitable,
for he must have felt that the situations of the story offered abundant opportunities
for the composition of pure lyric music, in which he excelled. The tragedy of

"Romeo and Juliet" had tempted many opera-composers before Gounod. Among them may be mentioned Dalayrac, Steibelt, Zingarelli, Vaccai, Bellini, and Marchetti, while Hector Berlioz had made it the subject of a dramatic symphony. The librettists of "Faust", Jules Barbier and Michael Carré, arranged the book, which some dramatic critics have praised as being an admirable adaptation of Shakespeare's play. Mlle. de Bovet, a French biographer of Gounod, has very sensibly said, however, that "all Jules Barbier's cleverness could not make the plot other than a love-duet, or rather a succession of love-duets".

While this is true, it is also a fact that the libretto presents the salient incidents of Shakespeare's tragedy in a compact and well-connected manner. In the endeavor to increase the number of parts for young women singers, the librettists introduced Stephano, the page, a character not found in the original play, and having no necessary connection with the story.

They may be forgiven this concession to the demands of operatic tradition, for the sake of the other excellences of their work. Gounod's music has been censured for its monotony, and the critics have generally agreed that this is due to the continual love-duet. A more pointed criticism is that which notes the similarity in the general style of these love-passages to those in "Faust". This similarity cannot well be questioned, and it forces comparisons which are not favorable to the music of "Romeo and Juliet". The love-scenes in "Faust" are the products of genuine inspiration, and they rise to a level of real greatness, seldom attained by the music of "Romeo and Juliet".

In regard to this aspect of the work, M. Arthur Pougin has well said: "If one wished to enter into what might be called a psychological analysis of the score, it would be necessary to discover how great were the difficulties of the composer in writing 'Romeo' without repeating himself, after having written 'Faust'. For, although the subjects of the two works differ widely, we see the same situations reproduced in each, under the same scenic conditions, and the stumbling-block was all the more troublesome, since these situations were the most salient ones, and constituted, as it were, the very core of the dramatic action. Witness the balcony-scene of 'Romeo' and the garden-scene of 'Faust', or the duel of Romeo and Tybalt, with the death of the latter in the first, and the duel of Faust and Valentine, also mortal, in the second. Truly, a musician must have a singular power, a very remarkable faculty of reiteration, to attempt, successfully, such a repetition of similar episodes"

Gounod was not the only man of high ability who attempted to do a second time what he had done at first to perfection. His failure to equal his first performance is certainly a demonstration of the limited power of his imagination; but, outside of the ranks of geniuses of the first order, such as Shakespeare and Goethe, no one has produced a second work so similar in character to a first, and yet so crowded with new beauties, as Gounod did in his "Romeo and Juliet". It is, beyond dispute, an opera of genuine and notable beauty. In the hands of artists, this work never fails to touch the heart of public enthusiasm; and in America, it has certainly grown greatly in favor since, in recent years, it has been performed by a company of singers of the first rank.

It would be uncomplimentary to the reader to tell the familiar story of "Romeo and Juliet", but it is necessary to outline it as it is given in the libretto of Barbier and Carré. The prelude contains a scene in which all the characters are grouped on the stage, and reference is made to the unhappy feud between the houses of Montague and Capulet. The first act takes place in the home of the Capulets. A ball is in progress in honor of Juliet's début in society. Juliet is formally introduced by her father, and subsequently expresses her happiness in the vocal waltz. To the ball, as maskers, come Romeo, Mercutio, and some of their friends. The first meeting of Romeo and Juliet takes place, and love at first sight follows. The appearance of Tybalt, who recognizes Romeo, gives rise to some dialogue, revealing to the lovers the identity of their respective families. Romeo and his friends leave the ball.

In the second act, we have the familiar balcony-scene of the Shakespearean drama. The interview of the lovers is briefly interrupted by the passage of the watch, whose suspicions of the presence of a stranger in the grounds are put to rest by the nurse. The love-scene then continues till the fall of the curtain. In the following scene, Romeo and Juliet go to the cell of Friar Laurence, and are married. In the third act, the feud between the two houses breaks out. Stephano, Romeo's page, fights with Tybalt, and Mercutio also fights with him, and is slain. Tybalt tries to force a quarrel with Romeo, but he declines the combat, until he is impelled to take vengeance for the death of Mercutio, his kinsman. Then he kills Tybalt, and is instantly overcome with horror and remorse, because Tybalt is Juliet's cousin. The Duke arrives upon the scene, and Capulet lays his complaint before him. The Duke sentences Romeo to exile, but the young man declares that he prefers death.

The rising of the curtain on the fourth act discovers Romeo and Juliet together in Juliet's chamber. Their love-scene is ended by the breaking of day, and Romeo is compelled to depart. Capulet enters and informs his daughter that he has chosen for her a husband, the Count Paris. In despair, she asks the aid of the Friar, who is present. He gives her a phial containing a drug to put her in a condition closely resembling death. The final scene shows us Juliet in her tomb. Romeo, returning to seek her, finds her, as he believes, dead. He slays himself, but before he breathes his last, Juliet revives, and the lovers join in one final outburst of despairing love before both die. It will be seen from this outline that the librettists succeeded in preserving the entire tragic action of the original play, while omitting the lighter scenes, such as those of Juliet with her mother and the nurse.

It is not necessary to enter into a detailed consideration of the music, which is very well able to speak for itself. In the first act, the most melodious and pleasing numbers are the solo of Capulet, the song of Mercutio describing Queen Mab, Juliet's waltz-song, and the first duet of the lovers. The waltz-song is a mere exhibition-aria, altogether out of place, and inserted only out of deference to a long-established custom. The second act consists almost wholly of the balcony-scene, and here Gounod's ability as a lyric writer is delightfully displayed. The music is, perhaps, a little too sentimental and not sufficiently passionate, but it is melodious and poetic. In the next scene, there is nothing remarkable, though the passage sung after the wedding usually pleases the hearers.

The following scene, in which Mercutio and Tybalt are killed, leans somewhat toward the style of Meyerbeer, but it lacks the theatrical vigor of that composer. On the other hand, the declamatory air of the tenor at its close is one of Gounod's most effective passages. In the fourth act, the composer is indeed at home, and here we meet with the most satisfying music of the opera. The duet, "Non, ce n'est pas le jour", is a finely dramatic piece of composition, and ranks with the best products of its writer's imagination. In the remainder of the opera, the only things to which especial attention need be called, are the charming orchestral accompaniment to Friar Laurence's announcement of his plan to save Juliet—heard again when she sleeps in the tomb—and the final love-duet.

"Roméo et Juliette" was produced at the Théâtre Lyrique, Paris, April 27, 1867, with Mme. Miolan-Carvalho as Juliet, and M. Michot as Romeo. The role of Juliet has been one of Mme. Adelina Patti's favorites, but the best cast of "Romeo and Juliet" in recent times, and probably the best ever brought together, was that of the Metropolitan Opera House at the opening of the season of 1894–95. It consisted of Mme. Melba as Juliet, Mlle. de Vigne as Stephano, Mlle. Bauermeister as the Nurse, M. Jean de Reszké as Romeo, M. Edouard de Reszké as Friar Laurence, M. Plançon as Capulet, Signor Gromzeski as Mercutio, M. Castelmary as the Duke, and M. Mauguiere as Tybalt.

W. J. HENDERSON.

Index.

Romeo and Juliet.

Overture-Prologue

with Chorus.

CHARLES GOUNOD.

*) This Chorus is to be sung by all the artists who interpret the *soli* of this score.

13203

naî - tre leurs a - mours!
a - ges could re - move!

naî - tre leurs a - mours!
a - ges could re - move!

naî - tre leurs a - mours!
a - ges could re - move!

Act I.

Nº 1. The Capulets' Ball.

Introduction.

10

SOPRANOS.

p

L'heu - re s'en - vo - le Joy - euse et
Swift hours of plea - sure Pass to gay

TENORS.

p

L'heu - re s'en - vo - le Joy - euse et
Swift hours of plea - sure Pass to gay

BASSES.

fol - le, Au pas - sage il faut la sai - sir,
mea - sure, Oh, en - joy them, while on they fly!

fol - le, Au pas - sage il faut la sai - sir,
mea - sure, Oh, en - joy them while on they fly!

13203

Cueil - lons les ro - ses Pour nous é - clo - ses Dans __ la __
Ros - es are blush - ing, Fair fac - es flush - ing, Why __ for -

Cueil - lons les ro - ses Pour nous é - clo - ses Dans la
Ros - es are blush - ing, Fair fac - es flush - ing, Why for -

joie __ et dans le __ plai - sir. __
bear, when all may en - joy? __

joie __ et dans le plai - sir. __
bear, when all may en - joy? __

12

13208

sem - ble Sont les hô - tes de ce pa - lais!___
maz - ing Are with - in this pal - ace to - day!___

Tybalt.

Vous n'en voy-ez pas la mer - veil - le, Le tré - sor u - nique et sans
But as yet no note hast thou tak - en Of the rar - est trea - sure we

Paris.

prix, Qu'on des - tine à l'heureux Pâ - ris.___ Si mon cœur en -
own, That is___ des - tin'd for thee a - lone!___ If naught yet my

co - re som-meil-le, Le moment est proche où l'a - mour Viendra l'éveil-ler à son
heart could a - wak-en, Now the time is near that shall move It to a - wak-en un-to

Tybalt.

tour.___ Il s'é - veil - le - ra,___ il s'é - veil - le - ra, je l'es-pè -
love!___ It shall yet a - wake,___ it shall yet a - wake, or I won -

Lo stesso movimento.

re:
der:

Re - gar - dez!____
On - ly see!____

re - gar - dez!   la voi - ci, con - dui - te   par   son
on - ly see!   by   the   hand her fa - ther leads her

pè - re.
yon - der!

cresc.- - - -

f   p

Capulet.   **Moderato** ($\quad$=76)

Soy - ez les bien - ve -
I bid ye wel - come

nus, a - mis____ dans ma mai - son!____   À   cet - te fè - te de fa -
all, my friends, within my home!____   This   is   a joy - ful cel - e -

p

mil — le, La joie est de sai — son, la joie est de sai —
bra — tion, This day whereon ye come, this day where-on ye

son! _____ Pa — reil jour vit naî — tre ma fil — le! Mon cœur bat de plai —
come! _____ And my heart beats high in e — la-tion, For on this day was

cresc.

sir en-core _____ en y son-geant! Mais ex — cu — sez ma ten-dresse in-dis —
born my on — ly daughter dear! Par-don, I pray you, a fa-ther's fond

dim. p

crê — te _____ Voi — ci _____ ma Ju — li — et — te! Ac-cueil-lez —
heart! _____ You see _____ my daughter Ju — liet! May you re —

la d'un re-gard in-dul — gent.
gard her in-dul-gent-ly here!

Andante. (♩=54)

pp

Ped. *

13203

Allegro.
Ah! qu'elle est bel - le! qu'elle est bel - le!
Ah! she is charm-ing! she is charm - ing!
TENORS.
Ah! qu'elle est bel - le! qu'elle est bel - le!
Ah! she is charm-ing! she is charm - ing!
BASSES.
Allegro. (𝅗𝅥=60.)
cresc. molto
Juliet.
É - cou - tez! é - cou - tez! C'est le son des in - stru - ments joy - eux Qui nous ap - pelle et nous con - vi - e! Ah!
On - ly hear! On - ly hear! How the tones air - i - ly ring and rise! How they in - vite, woo - ing - ly blend - ing! Ah!
cresc.

Tout_____ un monde en____ -chan-
All_____ a - round fai- -ry-

té sem- -ble naître à mes yeux!__
land seems to ra - vish mine eyes!__

Tout___ me fê- -te et____ m'en i- -vre,
Danc- -ers wend- -ing, Gal- -lants bend- -ing,

Tout_ me_ fête et m'en i- -vre!
In_ one_ vi- sion un- -end- -ing!

cresc. - - -

dim. p

Nar - gue! nar-gue des_ cen - seurs, Qui gron-dent, qui
Down them, down them, grum - blers all,_ Who're chid - ing, who're

gron - dent, qui gron - dent sans ces-se! Fê - tez la_ jeu - nes - se! Fê -
chid - ing, who're chid - ing for_ ev-er! Fair youth is_ in_ fa - vor, fair

tez la_ jeu - nes-se! Fê - tez la_ jeu-nes-se, Et place aux dan-
youth is_ in_ fa - vor, fair youth is_ in_ fa - vor! Make way_ for the

seurs!_
ball!_

Qui reste à sa place Et ne dan - se pas, De quelque dis-
An - y la - dy here Who is dain - ty now, She doth wear a

grâ-ce Fait l'a-veu tout bas! Qui reste à sa place Et ne dan-se
corn Up-on her toe, I vow! An-y la-dy here Who is dain-ty

pas, De quel-que dis-grâ-ce Fait l'a-veu tout bas! Ô re-gret ex-
now, She doth wear a corn Up-on her toe, I vow! By'r La-dy! My

trê-me! Quand j'é-tais moins vieux, Je gui-dais moi-mê-me Vos é-bats jo-
day for a mea-sure is gone, Tho' gal-lant more gay nev-er vis-or put

yeux! Les dou-ces pa-ro-les Ne me coutaient rien! Que
on! To la-dy's ear oft I a love-tale would tell, And

d'a-veux fri-vo-les Dont je me sou-viens!
whis-per-ing soft, I could please her right well!

Nar - gue! nar - gue! des___ cen - seurs, Qui gron-dent, qui
Down them, down them, grum-blers all,___ Who're chid - ing, who're

gron-dent, qui gron-dent sans ces-se! Fê - tez la_ jeu - nes-se! Fê -
chid-ing, who're chid-ing for_ ev-er! Fair youth is_ in_ fa-vor, fair

tez la_ jeu - nes-se! Fê - tez la_ jeu-nes-se, Et place aux dan-
youth is_ in_ fa - vor, fair youth is_ in_ fa-vor! Make way_ for the

seurs, Et place aux dan - seurs, Et pla-___-ce
ball,_ make way_ for the ball,_ make way___

aux___ dan - seurs!___
for___ the ball!___

a tempo.

place _____ aux _____ dan - seurs!_____
way _____ for _____ the ball!_____

place _____ aux _____ dan - seurs!_____
way _____ for _____ the ball!_____

Nº 1 bis. Scene.

Mercutio. En-fin la place est libre, a - mis!____
My friends, we are a - lone, at last!____

Romeo. Non, non, vous l'a - vez pro-
No, no, for your word you

Pour un in - stant____qu'il soit per-mis d'ô-ter son masque.
Now I may doff____ my vis - or for a mo-ment on - ly.

mis! Soy-ons pru-dents! i - ci____ nul ne doit nous con-naî-tre!
pass'd! Let us be - ware, for here____ to be known were dis-as - ter!

Quittons cet - te mai-son sans en bra-ver le mai____-tre.
Now let us leave the house be - fore we brave its mas____-ter.

Mercutio. Bah!____
Bah!____

34

si les Ca - pu-lets sont gens à se fà - cher, C'est là - che-té de nous ca -
If they think we came to quar- rel or de ride, We should be cow'rd if we to

Tempo moderato. *ben ritmato.*

cher, Car nous a-vons tous là de quoi leur te-nir tê - te!
hide; For ev-'ry man of us has where-with-al to curb them!

Oui, nous a-vons tous là de quoi leur te-nir tê - te! ___
Ay, ev-'ry man of us has where-withal to curb them! ___

6 TENORS.

Oui, nous a-vons tous là de quoi leur te-nir tê - te! ___
Ay, ev-'ry man of us has where-withal to curb them! ___

6 BASSES.

Oui, nous a-vons tous là · de quoi leur te-nir tê - te! ___
Ay, ev-'ry man of us has where-withal to curb them! ___

№ 2. Ballade of Queen Mab.

nais, sub-ti - le den - telle, Ont e - té dé-cou - pés dans l'ai -
top a grass-hop-per's wing, And a this-tle-down spring! Her driv -

le De quel - que ver - te sau-te - rel - le Par son co -
er, A small grey gnat, he made the cov - er, That she may

cher, le mou-che - ron! Un os de gril - lon sert de
lie well in the shade. A film is the lash of her

manche À son fouet,___ dont la mè - che blanche Est
whip, And the stock,___ is a crick-et - bone; 'Twas

prise au ra - yon qui s'é - panche De Phœ-bé ras-sem - blant___ sa
wound from the rays of the moon When high it shone in the sky___ a-

cour.
bove.

Cha - que nuit, dans cet é - qui -
Ev - 'ry night, so aïr - i - ly

pa - ge, Mab vi - si - te, sur son pas - sa - ge, L'époux qui rê - ve de - veu -
car - ried, Mab doth wan - der, and where she's tarried The spouse will dream that he's - un -

vage__ Et l'a - mant qui rê - ve d'a - mour! À son ap - pro - che, la__ co -
mar - ried, And the lov - er dreameth of love! And the co - quette, when Mab is

quet - te Re - ve d'a - tours et de toi - let - te, Le cour - ti - san fait la cour -
near - ing, Dreams of ap - par - el gay she's wear - ing, Suitors to bow dream of pre -

bet - te, Le po - è - te ri - me ses vers!__ A l'a -
par - ing, And the rime-ster rim - eth his rime!__ Then the

13203

vare en son gî - te som - bre, Elle ou - vre des tré - sors_____ sans
mi - ser, in sor - did slum - ber, Sees rich - es more than he_____ can

nom - bre, Et là li - ber - té rit dans l'ombre Au pris-on-
num - ber, And the pris-on-cell chill and som - bre, Brightens in

nier char-gé de fers._____ Le sol - dat rê - ve d'embus-
free-dom's ray sub - lime!_____ And the sol-dier dreams of am-bus-

pp

ca - des, De ba - tail - les et d'es-to-ca -
cades,_ Of healths five fath - om deep, and Span-ish blades,_____

des, El - le lui ver - se les ra-sa - des Il e
_____ Wak - en'd by roar-ing can-non-ades_____ He

poco ritardando.

poco ritardando.

Nº 2 bis. Recit. and Scene.

er Ton fol a - mour d'é - co - lier!__ Viens!
ny Your fool-ish love, sil-ly boy!__ Come!

Allegro. (♩=96)

Romeo.   Moderato.

Ah! voy-
Ah! be-

Romeo.

ez!__ Cet-te beau-té cé - les - te Qui semble un rayon dans la
hold!__ Yon-der ce - les - tial beau - ty, That beams like a ray in the

Mercutio.

Qu'est-ce donc?
What is yon?

Mercutio.

nuit!__ Le por - te - re-spect qui la suit__ Est d'u - ne beau-
night!__ But hard - ly so charm-ing a sight__ Is the guard of

48

(laughing)

Ah! ah!   Je son - ge
Ah! ah!   My mind on

Vous au-rez là, dit-on, la per-le des ma-ris.
A ver-y flow'r! A flow'r! How hap-py shall you   be!

bien vraiment au ma - ri - a - ge!
such a dream nev-er has tar-ried!

Par ma ver - tu! j'é-tais ma - ri -
Why la - dy mine! When I was your

Non! non!_ je ne veux pas t'é-cou-ter plus long-
No! no!_   I will no more hear the song you would

ée à_votre à - ge!
age, I_was mar - ried!

temps! Lais-se mon â - me, lais-se mon âme_ à son prin -
sing! O, let my heart,_ O, let my heart_ re-joice in

19203

Nº 3. Arietta.

Ce___ jour___ en_ _cor!__ Dou -
Yet___ one___ day___ more! Like

ce flam_ _me,_____ Je te
a trea_ _sure____ I will

gar_ _de___ dans mon a_ _
guard___ thee,___ naught my plea_

me___ Com_ _me un tré - sor!_____ Je
sure___ E'er____ will re - store!___ In

veux vi_ _vre___ Dans ce rè -
my fai_ _ry___ Dream I'd rev_ _

veux vi - vre___ Dans ce rê-
my fai - ry___ Dream I'd rev-

ve___ qui m'en i - vre___ Long -
el,___ gay and air - y,___ Yet___

temps en - cor! Dou - ce flam
one day more! Like a trea

me,___ Je te gar - de___
sure___ I will guard___ thee,___

dans mon â - me___ Com - me un tré-
naught my plea - sure___ E'er___ will re-

Un poco meno allegro, ma poco.

sor! Loin__ de l'hi - ver mo - ro - se, Lais - se
store! Far__ from the win - ter snows, Do not

moi,_____ lais - se moi som - meil - ler, Et__ res - pi -
wake,_____ do not wake me to - day; Let__ me en -

rer la ro - se, res - pi - rer la rose A - vant
joy the rose, Let me en - joy the rose Ere she

Tempo I.

de lef - feuil - ler. Ah!_____ Ah!_____
with - er a - way! Ah!_____ Ah!_____

Ah!_____ Ah!_____
Ah!_____ Ah!_____

Comme un tré - sor   Long - - - temps__ en - cor! _____
Naught will re - store   When _____ thou__ art   o'er! _____

a tempo.

Nº 3 bis. Recit.

Nº 4. Madrigal

à due.

mè - me, Pour - vu qu'il ai - me, Ont d'a - van - ce par-don-
hear him, Ere he im-plore them, If his heart know love di-

né.— Mais à sa bou-che La main qu'il
vine.— Yet, as a fa - vor, Fair hand may

tou-che Prudem - ment doit re-fu - ser_____ Cet - te ca-
nev-er To his lip its will re-sign;_____ Tho' he con-

resse_ En - chan-te - res - se Qu'il im-plo- - re en un bai-
fess - es, His fond ca - ress-es, Win no leave_____ to kiss the

Romeo.

ser!_____ Les sain - tes ont pour-tant
shrine!_____ The saints have lips as well,

Romeo.

E - xau - cez donc mes vœux__ et gar - dez im-pas-si-ble Vo-
Oh, hear my ar - dent vow!__ And tho' blush-es may dark-en, Still__

rit.

Tempo I. (*molto determinato*)

Juliet.

Ah!__ je n'ai pu m'en dé - fen - dre! J'ai pris
Ah!__ I've no pow'r to re - fuse it! Now my

molto.

- tre front rou-gis - sant!
__un-mov'd be your brow!

Tempo I. (*molto determinato*)

Romeo.

le pé - ché pour moi!__ Pour a - pai - ser vo-tre é - moi!__ Vous plaît-
own the sin shall be!__ Mine let the sin ev - er be!__ Give it

Juliet. *cresc.* **Romeo.**

il de me le ren - dre? Non! je l'ai pris! lais - sez - le moi! Vous
me, and you will lose it! No! it is mine! Ah, leave it me! No!

№ 5. Finale.

Adagio. **Juliet.** (terrified).

'Cé - tait Ro - mé - o!
'Twas Ro - meo him - self!

(absorbedly, with fixed gaze)

Ah!___ je l'ai vu trop tôt___ sans le con-
Ah!___ Too ear-ly seen un-known, and known too

naî - tre!
late!___

La haine est le ber-ceau de cet a-mour fa-
Fell ha - tred is the cra-dle of this fa - tal

tal!___
love!___

C'en est fait!___
Woe is me!___

si je ne puis être à
If I nev - er his may

lui,___
be,___

Que le cer-cueil soit mon lit nup - ti -
For me the grave, then a bride - bed shall

Tybalt.
Pati - en - ce! pati - en - ce! De cet-te mortelle of - fen - se Romé-
Only pa - tience!only pa - tience!This mortal affront, I swear it, Yonder

o, j'en fais ser - ment, Su - bi - ra le châ-ti - ment!___
slave, so prone to strife, Soon shall an - swer with his life!___

Mercutio.
On nous ob -
See how they

ser - ve, si - len - ce! Il faut u - ser de pru-den-ce! N'at-tendons
watch us! Be si - lent, And rather pru - dent than violent! Let us not

Capulet.
pas fol - le - ment___ Un fu - neste é - vè - ne - ment. Que la
wait in a - maze___ Till the house be in a blaze! Rouse a -

fè - te re - com-men-ce! Que l'on boive et___ que l'on dan - se! Au - tre-
gain the sound of pleasure!Drain the wine-cup,tread the measure! Time has

fois, j'en fais ser-ment, Nous dan-sions plus vail-lam-ment, Nous dan-
been, I swear to you, When I danc'd and drank for two, when I

sions plus vail - lam - ment, Nous dan - sions plus vail - lam-
danc'd and drank for two, when I danc'd and drank for

cresc.

ment!
two!

SOPRANOS. *f*
Que la fê - te re - com-men-ce! Que l'on boive et que l'on
Rouse a - gain the sound of pleasure! Drain the wine-cup, tread the

TENORS. *f*
Que la fê - te re - com-men-ce! Que l'on boive et que l'on
Rouse a - gain the sound of pleasure! Drain the wine-cup, tread the

BASSES. *f*
Que la fê - te re - com-men-ce! Que l'on boive et que l'on
Rouse a - gain the sound of pleasure! Drain the wine-cup, tread the

f   *f*

Chorus.

74

Je te dé - fends___ de faire un pas!___
And I for - bid you to take a step!___

Al - lons! jeunes gens! Al - lons! belles da-mes!Aux
A hall, mer-ry men! A hall, bonny ladies! Who

plus___di - li - gents Ces yeux pleins de___ flammes! Ces yeux, ces
will___not___be___ won___ Where beau-ty___ ar - ray'd is, Be won, where

yeux pleinsde___ flam - mes! Nar - gue! nar - gue des___ cen -
beau-ty___ar - ray'd___ is? Down them, down them, grum - blers

seurs, Qui grondent, qui grondent, qui gron-dent sans ces-se! Fê-
all,__ Who're chid-ing,who're chid-ing,who're chid-ing for__ ev-er! Fair

tez la__ jeu-nes-se! Fê-tez la__ jeu-nes-se! Fê-tez la__ jeu-
youth is__ in__ fa-vor, fair youth is__ in__ fa-vor, fair youth is__ in__

nes-se, Et place aux dan-seurs, Et place aux dan-seurs, Et
fa-vor!Make way__for the ball,__ make way__for the ball,__ make

pla- -ce aux_____ dan-seurs!_____
way_____ce for_____the ball!_____

aux _____ dan - seurs! _____
for _____ the ball! _____

aux _____ dan - seurs! _____
for _____ the ball! _____

aux _____ dan - seurs! _____
for _____ the ball! _____

a tempo

ff

End of Act I.

Act II.

The Garden of Juliet.

№ 6. Entr'acte and Chorus.

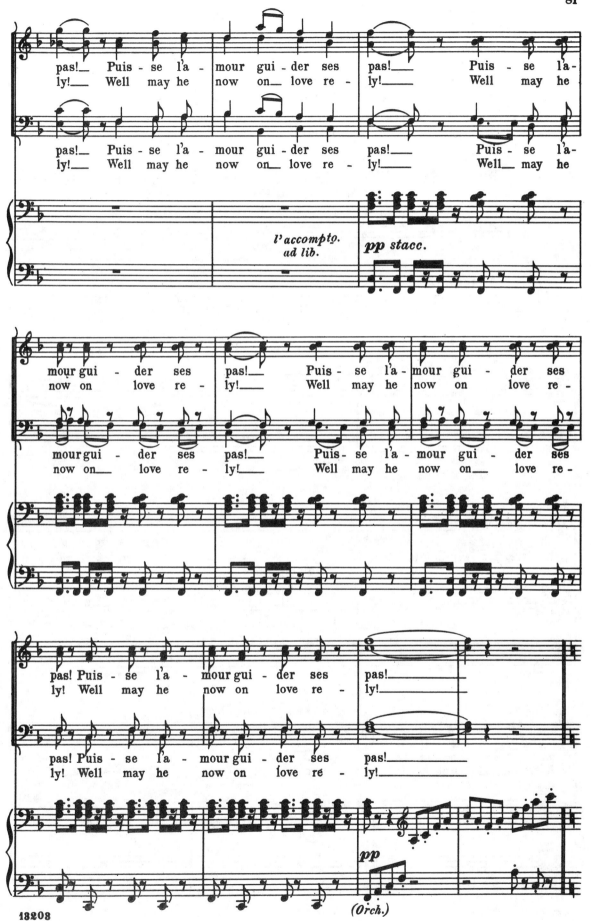

№ 7. Cavatina.

Romeo. La-mour! la-mour! oui,__ son ar - deur a troublé tout mon
On love! On love! Ay, for my heart in his bondage is

Piano.

Adagio. (♩=52.)

ê - tre! Mais quel - le sou - dai - ne clar - té re - splen-
aching! But what sud - den light doth mine eye now be-

dit à cet - te fe - nê - tre? C'est là que dans la
hold thro'yon win-dow breaking? The ray of morn-ing

L'istesso tempo. (♪=50.)

nuit ray - on - ne sa beau - té!
'tis, and Ju - liet is the sun!

Nº 8. Scene and Choruses.

o! dis-moi loy-a-le-ment:_ je t'ai-me! Et je te
love! If on-ly thou wilt say:_ "I love thee!" I will be-

crois!_ et mon hon-neur se fie au tien, O mon sei-
lieve!_ and will con-fide my soul to thine; Oh, thou my

gneur!_ com-me tu peux te fi-er_ à moi mê-
lord!_ on me re-ly as on Heav-en a-bove_

me! N'ac-cu-se pas mon cœur, dont tu sais le se-cret,_ D'è-tre lé-
thee! Yet lay not an-y blame on my heart, I en-treat,_ Nor deem me

poco riten, ma poco.

ger pour n'a-voir pu se tai-re_ Mais ac-cu-se la nuit, dont le voile indis-
light, be-cause of love o'er-lav-ish; Lay all blame on the night, that with veil indis-

Chorus.

Più moderato.

Gertrude.

De qui par-lez-vous donc?
Who is he you be - rate?

Gregorio.

D'un pa - ge Des Montai -
A page Of Mon-ta-gue's

Più moderato.

p.

gus! Maître et va - let En pas - sant no - tre
house! Mas - ter and man In o'er - pass-ing our

seuil ont o - sé faire ou - trage Au sei - gneur Ca - pu -
thresh - old have thrown down a gage To the head of our

Gertrude.

Vous mo - quez - vous?
Are you in jest?

let! Non! sur ma tè - te!
clan! No! Give at - ten - tion!

f

№ 9. Duet.

Juliet.

Romeo.

Andante.

Ô nuit di-vi-ne! je t'im-plo-re, lais-se mon cœur à ce reve enchan-
Oh night of rapture! I im-plore thee, still leave my heart in this dream of de-

Piano.

pp

té!__ Je crains de m'éveil-ler et n'o-se croire en-core à sa ré-a-li-
light! I fear I shall a-wake! I may not dare as yet be-lieve in it a-

pp

Juliet.

Moderato.

Ro-mé-o!__ Art thou here?

té! right!

Un seul mot__ But a word:

Douce a-mi-e! My be-lov-ed!

Moderato.

p

Tempo.
solemnly

puis a-dieu! then good-night!

Quel-qu'un i-ra demain te trou-ver:__ sur ton
To-mor-row I shall send un-to thee:__ By all that is

je te l'ai dit, je t'a - do - - re! Dis - si - pe ma
I say a - gain, I a - dore thee! Dis - pel thou my

nuit!_ sois l'au - ro - re, sois l'au - rore Où va mon
night!_ Send be - fore thee, Send be - fore thy rays, oh

cœur, où vont mes yeux!_____ Dis - pose en
sun, re - joice mine eyes!_____ My heart can

rei - ne, dis - po - se de ma vi - e,
on - ly de - sire what - e'er thou will - est,

Verse à mon âme i - nas-sou - vi - - e, Verse___
Thou all my soul with rap-ture fill - - est, thou___

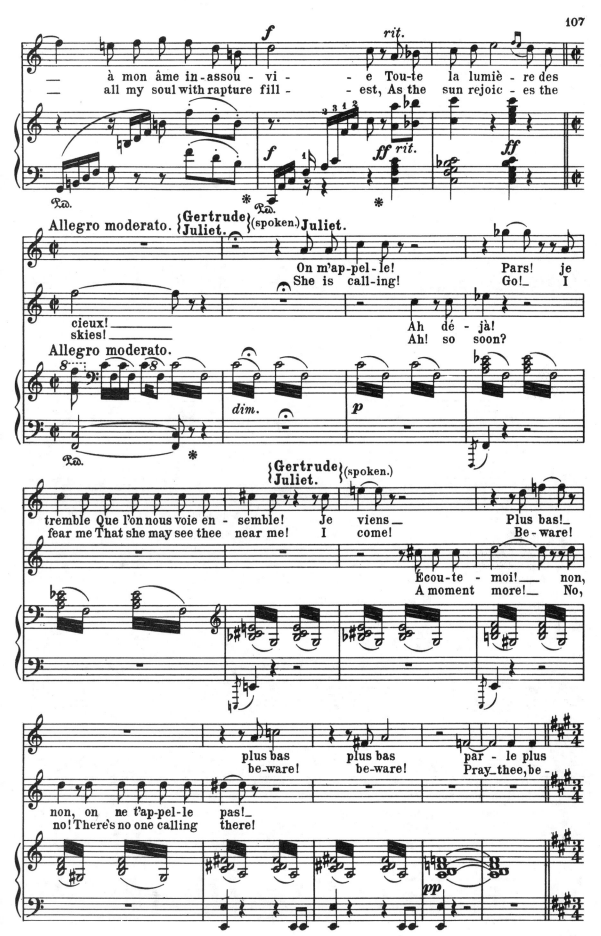

Dou - ce - ment vien - ne se po - ser!
May the smile for thy lov - er be,

Et mur-mur-ant en - cor: Je t'aime! à ton o - reil - le Que la
Murm'-ring a - gain, "I love thee!" A-gain near thee in seem - ing! May the

poco rit. *a tempo.*

bri - se des nuits te por - te ce bai - ser!
breez - es of night bear on my kiss to thee!

poco rit. *a tempo.*

(curtain.)

p *pp*

End of Act II.

The Cell of Friar Laurence.

№ 10. Entr'acte and Scene.
1st Tableau.

pè - re! Dieu vous gar - de!   Dieu vous gar - de!
mor-row, ho - ly Fa -ther!   Fair good mor - row!

F. Laurence.
Recit.

Eh! quoi! le jour à pei - ne Se lè - ve. et le sommeil te
How now? The day but hard - ly is break-ing, And slum-ber flees thine

Recit.

fuit?_ Quel trans-port vers moi te con - duit?_ Quel amoureux sou-ci t'a-
eye?_ Why to me so ear-ly dost hie?_ What cares of love com-pel thy

_p_ ＜   cresc.   dim.

mè - ne?
wak - ing?

Romeo.

Vous l'avez de-vi - né, mon pè - re, c'est l'a-
You di-vine it a - right, my Fa - ther; it is

_p_   _f_   dim.

mour!__
love!__

Quel nom prononcez_
That name I have for-

L'amour!   en - cor   l'in-di-gne Ro - sa - li - ne.
'Tis love!   A - gain th'un-wor-thy Ro - sa - line?__

p

f

Moderato e misurato.

vous?   je ne le connais   pas!__
got,   and with it   all my   woe!__

L'œil
When,

des é-
borne on

f

f

pp

Ped.

lus,_____   sou - vrant   à la clar-té di - vi - ne,
high,_____   the   soul   a-wakes in light di - vine,_____

Ped.   Ped.   Ped.   Ped.

Se   souvient-il   en - cor_____   des   om-bres d'i-ci-
Can   it re-mem-ber   still_____   the   gloom left here be-

Ped.   Ped.   Ped.

124

Voi-ci mon é - poux!— Vous connais-sez ce cœur que je lui
be-hold— my spouse!— You know this heart that un-to him I

don - ne! À son amour je m'aban - don - - ne; Devant le
prof - fer! Un-to his love my life I of - - fer! In sight of

F. Laurence.

ciel u - nis-sez — nous!— Oui! dus-sé-je affron-
heav'n hal-low our vows!— Ay! tho'blind be their

ter une a-veu-gle co-lè-re, Je vous prê-te-rai mon se-
ire when of-fense may be giv-en, I will lend my aid to you

13203

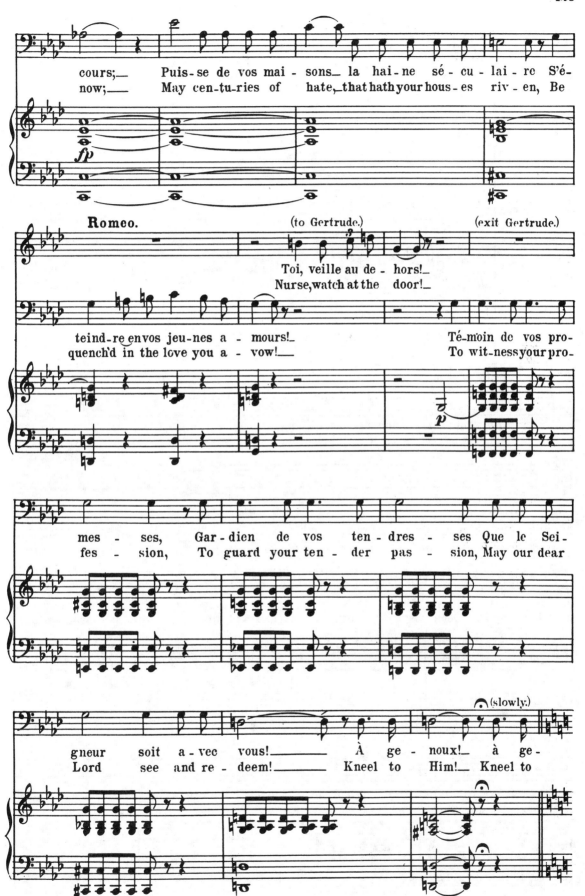

№ 11. Trio and Quartet.

Dieu,_qui fis l'homme à ton i - ma - - ge, Et de sa chair et de son
Thou,_who mad'st man in Thine own im - - age, And of his flesh and of his

sang cré-as la fem-me, Et, l'u-nissant à l'homme par le ma-ri-
blood cre-at-edst wo-man, And un-to him u - nit-edst her in bonds of

a - ge, Con-sa-cras du haut de Si - on Leur in-sé-pa-rable u - ni-
mar - riage, From Thy heav'n-ly man-sion a - bove Pu-ri-fy and hal - low their

joug d'amour et de paix!___ Que la ver-tu soit sa ri-
yoke of love un-al - loy'd!___ Ev - er may vir-tue be her

che - se, Que pour soute-nir sa fai - blesse Elle ar-me son cœur du de-
dow - er; Guid - ed and sustain'd by Thy pow'r May she in Thy fear e'er a-

Juliet.

Sei - gneur, sois mon ap - pui,___ sois mon es - poir!___
O Lord!___ E'er be my stay,___ e'er be my guide!___

Romeo.

voir!___ Sei - gneur, sois mon ap - pui,___ sois mon es - poir!___
bide!___ O Lord!___ E'er be my stay,___ e'er be my guide!___

F. Laurence.

Que leur viellesse heu - reuse___ voie Leurs en - fants marchant dans ta
May their old age be bless - ed, may Their chil-dren ev - er walk in Thy

134

Public square before the palace of the Capulets.

Nº 12. Chanson.
2ᵈ Tableau.

Stephano.

Recit. Moderato.

(eyeing the balcony of

De - puis hi - er   je cher - che en vain mon maî - tre!   Est - il en - core chez
Since yes - ter eve   I vain - ly seek my mas - ter.   Can he still be with -

the palace.)

misurato.

(arrogantly.)

vous, Mes - sei - gneurs Ca - pu - lets?_____   Voy - ons un peu si vos di - gnes va -
in with a foe that he hates?_____   Now let me see, Mes - sei - gneurs Cap - u -

lets   A ma voix ce ma - tin   o - se - ront re - pa - raî - tre!
lets,   If you dare walk a - broad   to re - pair your dis - as - ter!

Qui vi - vrà ve - drà!   Vo - tre__ tour te -
They who live shall__ see!   For your__ dain - ty

rel - le   Vous é - chap - pe - ra,
dar - ling   May one__ day go free,

Vo - tre__ tour te - rel - le__ Vous é - chap - pe -
For__ your__ dain - ty__ dar - ling__ May__ one__ day__ go

Tempo I.

ra!__   Un ra - mier, loin du vert bo -
free!__   Drawn by love, from his wood - land

ca - ge, Par l'a - mour at - ti - ré,__ À l'en -
hie - ing, Came a ring - dove that way,__ All a -

13203

tour de ce nid sau - va - ge A, je crois, sou - pi -
round yon-der ey - rie sigh - ing He did rove, so__they

poco animando

ré!____ Les vau - tours sont à la cu - ré - e, Leurs chan -
say!____ Lured a - field by a prey they're man - gling, Yet a -

p poco animando

sons que fuit Cy - thé - ré - e Ré - son - nent à grand
far the vul - tures are wran - gling, Their cries the ear af -

a tempo

bruit!_____ Ce - pen - dant, en leur douce i - vres - se Nos a -
fright!_____ And the while, fond - ly won in woo - ing, Lov - ers

a tempo

mants con-tent leur ten - dres - se Aux as - tres de la
twain ten - der - ly__ are coo - ing 'Neath wond'ring stars of

pp

attacca.

№ 13. Finale.

144

ce pour nous nar - guer, mon jeu - ne ca - ma - ra - de, Que
will you here, young friend? Are you for quar-rel_ yearning, That

vous nous ré - ga - lez de cet-te_ sé - ré - na - de?
you re - gale us with your song at_ ear-ly_morn - ing?

Stephano.

J'ai - me la mu - si - que!
I am fond of mu - sic!

C'est clair, c'est clair, On_ t'au -
'Tis clear, 't is clear, Your_ gui -

ra sur_ le_ dos, en pa-reille é-qui-pé - e, Cas-sé ta gui - ta - re, mon cher!
tar, for_ a_ like sil - ly prank, was_ bro-ken, And o-ver your shoulders, my dear!

13203

(Enter Tybalt, who answers the insult.)

di - gne des Ca - pu - lets! Tels maì - tres, tels va -
harms a Cap - u - let's name! Like mas - ter, like _

Tybalt (insolently.)

lets! Vous a - vez la pa - ro - le promp - te, mon - sieur!
man! With your tongue you are ver - y read - y, I vow!

Mercutio. **Tybalt.**

Moins promp - te que le bras!.. _ C'est ce qu'il fau - drait
My arm _ is read - ier still! _ Sore - ly you'll need it

Mercutio. (Mercutio and Tybalt engage;

voir!... _ C'est ce que tu ver - ras! _
now! _ Try me when-e'er you will! _

at the same instant, Romeo rushes in and tries to separate them.)

Toi dont la bou-che mau - di - te A Ju-li-ette in-ter-di - te O -
Thy curs-ed lip e-ven near-ing Sli-ly to Ju-li-et's hear-ing, Where

a tempo (disdainfully.)

sa, je crois,_ par-ler tout bas, É - cou-te le seul mot que m'ins -
it were best_ for ev - er dumb! Now hear the on-ly name that my

colla voce *a tempo*

pi - re ma hai - ne! Tu n'es qu'un là - che!
hate can pre-sent thee! Thou art a vil - lain!

(Romeo seizes and half-draws

pausa lungissima.

his sword; after a moment's hesitation, he returns it to the scabbard.)

Andante. ($\bullet$ = 54.)

Romeo (contained and dignified.)

Al - lons! _____
Not so! _____

tu ne me con-nais pas, Ty-balt,
Ty - balt, thou know'st me not!

Et ton in-sulte est vai - ne! J'ai dans le
And all in vain thine in - sult! Here in my

cœur des rai-sons de _ t'ai - mer, _ Qui mal-gré
heart I have rea - sons to love thee, That, spite of

moi ____ me vien - nent dé-sar - mer. Je ne suis pas un
all, ____ dis-arm wak-en-ing ire. Vil-lain am I

Tybalt.

lâ - che! a - dieu! Tu crois peut-ètre Ob-te-nír le par-don de tes of-
none!_ Fare-well! Dost thou en-deav-or To move me to par-don thy of-

Romeo.

fen - ses? traî - tre! Je ne t'ai ja-mais of-fen-
fens - es? Nev - er! Ty - bait, I ne'er have of-

je ven-ge-rai ton in-ju - - re! Mi - sé - ra - ble Ty-
I will to hon-or re-store thee, And a-venge thee on

cresc. - -

Tybalt.

Je suis à
And with a

balt! en garde, et dé-fends - toi! _____
him! Now draw, foul-spo-ken Ty - balt!

molto

ff

toi! _____
will! _____ **Romeo.**

É - cou - te moi! _____
Will you not hear? _____

Mercutio.

Non lais-se - moi!.. _____
No! I will fight! _____

Chorus.
TENORS.

f

Bien sur ma foi! En lui j'ai
Good! he will fight, Nor bear a

BASSES.

f

Bien sur ma foi! En lui j'ai
Good! he will fight, Nor bear a

156

13203

160

(Tybalt and Mercutio engage.)

Romeo.

(to Tybalt, with a thrust.)

A toi!
Have at thee!

ff

fff

Capulet.

Grand Dieu! Ty - balt!!!
Oh Heav'ns! 'Tis Ty - balt!

fp

p

Benvolio.

Sa bles-sure est mor - tel - le! Fuis sans perdre un ins-
He is mor - tal - ly wound - ed! Hence! Be - gone while thou

SOPRANOS I & II. **Stephano** with SOPR. I.

TENORS. **Romeo** with 1st TENORS, **Benvolio** with 2nd TENORS.

BASSES. **Paris** with 1st BASSES, **Gregorio** with 2nd BASSES.

Ô jour de deuil! Ô jour de
O day of woe! O day of

lar - mes! Un a - veu - gle courroux Ensang-lan - te nos
weep - ing! Blind re-venge hath our blades In their blood now been

ar - - - - mes! Et le mal -
steep - - - - ing, And bale - ful

Rien ne pour-ra cal-mer les fur-reurs cri-mi - nel - les! Rien ne fe-ra tom-
Naught ev - er can al - lay the in - hu-man con - ten - tions! Naught ev - er can your

ber les ar - mes de vos mains, Et je se-rai moi-même at-teint par vos que-
war - ring hands for once dis - arm, And I may be my - self a prey to your dis-

(to Romeo)

rel - les! Se - lon nos lois, ton crime a mé-ri-té la
sen - sions! For thy of - fense, the for - feit of our law is

Romeo. Moderato maestoso.

Ciel!
Ban - ish'd!

mort.— Mais tu n'es pas l'a-gres - seur— Je t'ex - i - le!
death! But, as'twas he who be - gan,— thou art ban-ish'd!

Moderato maestoso.

The Prince. (to the Montagues and Capulets)

Et vous, dont la haine en pré-tex-tes fer-
And ye, who in hate ev - er prone to oc-

ti - le, En-tretient la dis - corde et l'ef-froi dans la
ca - sion, Do in-flame in our town wo-ful strife and ag-

vil - le, Prê - tez tous de-vant moi le serment so-len-
gres - sion, Swear ye all, on your lives, or at home or a-

nel_ D'o-bé - is-sance aux lois et du prince et du ciel!_
broad, Ye will o-bey the laws of the Prince and of God!_

Romeo.

Ah! jour de deuil_ et d'hor - reur_ et d'a-lar - mes,
Ah! dire - ful day,_ day of woe_ and of mourn - ing,

Mon cœur se brise é - per - du de dou - leur!____
Break - ing, my heart fails in pain and de - spair!____

In - juste ar - rêt qui trop tard nous dé - sar - mes,
Tho' we dis - arm, how un - time - ly the warn - ing!

Tu mets le comble à ce jour de mal - heur!____
For we may nev - er thy rav - age re - pair!____

Je vois pé - rir dans le sang et les lar - mes
Ev - 'ry de - sire, ev - 'ry hope grim - ly scorn - ing,

Tous les es - poirs et tous les vœux de mon
Weep - ing and blood a - lone in thee may we

End of Act III.

Act IV.

Nº 14. The Chamber of Juliet.
1st Tableau.
(It is still night.)
Duet.

mort! S'il n'a-vait succom-bé, tu suc-com-bais toi-mê-me! Loin de
blow; For if he were a-live, I should no lon-ger have thee! Naught of

moi la dou-leur!— loin de moi le re-mords! Il te ha-ïs-
sor-row I feel,— no re-morse do I know.— He did bear thee

Moderato.   **Romeo.**

sait— et je t'ai-me! Ah! re-dis-
hate,— and I love thee! Ah! yet a-

Juliet.

le,— re-dis-le,— ce mot si doux!— Je
gain,— yet a-gain re-peat thy vows!— I

t'ai-me,ô Ro-mé-o! je t'ai-me, Ô mon é-
love thee, oh my own! I love thee, oh my

188

Ô_____ douce nuit d'a-mour!_____ La des-ti
O_____ tender night di-vine!_____ Fate hath u-

Ô_____ douce nuit d'a-mour!_____ La des-ti
O_____ tender night di-vine!_____ Fate hath u-

né - - e M'en-chaî-ne à toi sans re - tour!_____
nit - - ed My heart for aye un - to thine!_____

né - - e M'en-chaî-ne à toi sans re - tour!_____
nit - - ed My heart for aye un - to thine!_____

Sous_____ tes bai - sers de flam - me Le
Glow - - ing in fond e - mo - tion The

Sous_____ tes bai - sers de flam - me Le
Glow - - ing in fond e - mo - tion The

cresc.

13203

do - re; De la nuit les flambeaux pâ - lis - - sent,
break - ing; Pal-lid nightwanes be - fore Au - ro - - - ra,

et l'au - ro - - re Dans les va-peurs de l'O - ri
who, a - wak - - ing, Veil'd in yon mist-y morn-ing

Juliet.

Tempo come prima.

Non!
No,

ent___ Se leve___ en sou - ri - ant!
skies,___ Doth smil - ing - ly a - rise!___

Tempo come prima.

p

non, ce n'est pas le jour,_____ cet - te lu - eur fu -
no! it is not the day,_____ Yon light so wan, so

p

nes - - te N'est que le doux re - flet___
drear - - y, Is but a pale re - flex___

p

du bel as - tre des nuits!_____ Res - te! res - te!
from the dim - beam - ing moon!_____ Tar - ry! Tar - ry!

pp cresc.

Romeo. Allegro. ff Recit.

Ah! vien - ne donc la
Ah! Be thou wel - come,

ff

Andante molto appassioato.

mort!_____ je res - te!
Death!_____ I tar - ry!

(con delirio.) ff

ff ff

(During this entire ritournelle, Juliet and Romeo remain entwined in each other's arms.)

cresc. molto.

pres - se   Et t'ar-ra-cher à cette ar-dente   i - vres - se!
fold thee,   Nor yet thy heart o-bey, that fain   would hold thee!

pres - se   Et l'ar-ra-cher à cette ar-dente   i - vres - se!
fold me,   Nor yet my heart o-bey, that fain   would hold me!

Ah! que le sort__ qui de toi__ me sé - pa - re,
Ah, fa - tal hour,__ that from thee__ me di - vid - eth,

Ah! que le sort qui de toi me sé - pa - re,
Ah, fa - tal hour, that from thee me di - vid - eth,

Plus que la mort__ est cru - el__ et bar - ba - re!
Thy cru - el pow'r__ more than death__ e'en be - tid - eth!

Plus que la mort est cru - el et bar - ba - re!
Thy cru - el pow'r more than death e'en be - tid - eth!

Il faut par - tir, hé-las!   Il faut quit - ter ces bras__ Où je te
Thou must in - deed a - way,   Nor in these arms de - lay__ Where I en -

Il faut par - tir, hé-las!   A - lors que dans ses bras__ El - le me
I must in - deed a - way,   Nor in these arms de - lay__ That now en -

(Juliet stands gazing fixedly at the balcony, over which Romeo has hastily departed.)

Andante. (♩ = 60) **Juliet.**

A - dieu! mon à - me! a - dieu ma vi - e!
Fare-well, be - lov-ed! May For-tune guide him!

(fervently.)

An - ges du ciel! à vous,___ à vous je le con -
An - gels of heav'n, to ye,___ to ye do I con -

fi - e!
fide___ him!

№ 15. Quartet.

Hé - las!___ no-tre souci, je le vois, est pa reil,___
A - las!___ Our lov-ing cares, as I see are the same,

Et les mê-mes re - grets___ hâ - tent no - tre ré - veil!
And our wak-en-ing thoughts own a like wo-ful aim!

Andantino. ($\bullet$ = 72)

Que l'hym - ne nup - ti - al___ suc - cède aux cris d'a-
A wed - ding song shall soon___ o'er - bear the wail of

Gertrude.

Cal-mez-vous! Cal-mez-vous!
Calm your-self! Calm your-self!

len - ce! Cal-mez-vous!
si - lent! Calm your-self!

Capulet.

L'au -
The

tel est pré-pa-ré,
al - tar is pre-pared,

Pâ - ris a ma pa-
the groom hath ap-pro-

ro - le, Soy-ez u - nis tous deux sans at-
ba - tion; Be ye u - nit - ed now, nor in-

tendre à de - main!
vite more de-lay!

Que l'om - bre de Ty-
May Ty - balt's wand'ring

balt,__ pré - sente à cet hy - men,__ S'a - pai - se, s'a-
shade,__ ap - prov - ing us to - day,__ Be laid then, be

paise en-fin et te con - so - - - - le.
laid in fi - nal con-so - la - - - - tion!

La vo - lonté des morts,__ com - me cel - le de Dieu lui - mê - me,
All wish-es of the dead,__ as the man-date of Him a - bove us,

Est u - ne loi sain - te, u - ne loi su - prê - me!
Like a ho - ly sum - mons to o - bey should move us:

Nous de-vons respec - ter___ la vo-lon - té des morts!___
May the dead rest in peace;___ let us re - gard their will!___

Juliet.
Ne crains rien,___ Ro - mé-o, mon cœur est sans re - mords!___
Fear thee not,___ Ro - me-o, my heart is faithful still!___

Gertrude.
Dans leur tom - be, dans leur tom - be
Let them slum - ber, let them slum - ber

Nous devons respec - ter___ la vo-lon - té des morts,___
May the dead rest in peace;___ let us re - gard their will,___

F. Laurence.
El - le trem - ble, El - le trem - ble,
She is trem - bling, she is trembling,

Ne crains rien, Ro - mé-o, mon cœur est sans re - mords,___ mon
Fear thee not, Ro - me-o, , my heart is faith-ful still,___ my

lais - sons en paix dor - mir les morts,___
well in their tomb, , nor dream of ill,___

Nous devons respec - ter___ la vo-lon - té des morts,___
may the dead rest in peace,___ let us re - gard their will,___

et mon cœur, mon cœur par-ta-ge ses re - mords,___ my
and my heart, my_ heart sad fore-bodings now fill,___ my

№ 16. Scene.

F. Laurence.

C'est là qu'après un jour vo - tre corps et votre â - me, Com-
And there, with-in a day, shall your heart feel a stri - ving, As

me d'un foyer mort se ra - ni - me la flam - me, Sor-ti - ront en-
when on chil-ly hearth for-mer flame_ is re - viv - ing, And your heav-y

fin de ce lourd som-meil; Par l'ombre pro-té - gés, votre é -
sleep you shall then for-sake! O'er-shadow'd by the night, with your

poux et moi - mê - me Nous é - pi - rons, nous é - pi - rons vo - tre ré -
spouse I'll e - spy you; We shall be nigh, we shall be nigh when you a -

veil___ Et vous fui - rez au bras de ce - lui qui vous ai - me,
wake,___ And you shall flee a - way with him whom they de - ny you,

13203

Et vous fui - rez au bras de ce - lui qui vous ai - me!
and you shall flee a - way with him whom they de - ny you!

Hé - si - tez - vous? Non!
Do you re - pent? No!

Juliet.

Moderato. *L'istesso movimento.*

non!__ à vo - tre main j'ab - ban - don - ne ma vi - e!
no!__ I will con - fide e - ven life to your keep - ing!

cresc. *f*

F. Laurence. **Juliet.** (firmly.) (Exit F. Laurence.)

À de - main!__ À de - main!__
For a day!__ For a day!__

dim.

Ballet.

Nº 17. Scene and Air.*)

Dieu! quel fris - son court dans mes vei - nes?
Heav'n! what a chill doth o - ver - run me!

*) At the Opera. this air is omitted.
13203

main pour-tant dans ce caveaux fu - nèbres Je m'éveillais avant son re-
mor - row morn, ere he re-turn, I wak - en, A - mid the lone-ly chill of the

tour? Dieu puissant!__ Cet - te pensée horrible a gla - cé tout mon
tomb: Heav'n - ly Pow'rs! This hor - ri - ble conceit chills the blood in my

Misurato. ($\textbf{♩} = 76$)

sang! Que deviendrai-je en ces té - nè - bres Dans se sé-jour de
veins! What should I do, lone and for - sak - en, In yon a-bode of

mort ____ et de gé-mis-se - ments, ____ Que les siècles pas-
death, ____ none near to heed my moans; ____ That the cen-tu-ries

sés ont rempli d'os - se - ments? Où Tybalt, tout sai-
past have re-plen - ish'd with bones? And wherein bloody

gnant en - cor_____ de sa bles - su - re, Près de moi, dans la nuit obs-
Ty - balt, fes - t'ring yet, is ly - ing, Close at hand in the gloom e-

cresc.

cu - re Dor - mi - ra! Dieu!!!_ ma main rencon - tre - ra sa
spy - ing, I should view_ Heav'ns!_ And if his hand were touching

(horrified.)

molto. *f* *fp*

main!____ Quelle est cette ombre à la mort é - chap-
mine.____ What is this shade, from the tomb grim-ly

(in bewilderment, as if seeing Tybalt's ghost.)

f *p*

pé - e? C'est Ty - balt!_ il m'ap-
gaz - ing? It is he!_ It is

f *p* *f* *p*

pel - le! il veut de mon che - min É - car - ter mon é - poux!_
Ty - balt! He calls me to de - part from the one whom I love!_

f *p* *cresc.*

Tempo I.

l'om-bre des tourments pas - sés! Viens!_____ A -
bove the gloom of woes gone by! Come!_____ Oh

mour!_____ ra - ni - me mon cou - ra - ge Et de mon
love!_____ revive my fond de - vo - tion, And from my

cœur chas - - se_ l'ef - froi!_____ Hé - si -
heart ban - - ish_ dis - may;_____ Now to

ter, c'est_____ te faire ou - tra - ge! Trem -
doubt, that_____ were to dis - own thee! To

bler,_____ est un man-que de foi! Ver - -
fear,_____ were my love to be - tray! Nev - -

End of Act IV.
(in ordinary stage-performance.)

№ 18. Nuptial Procession.

Allegro maestoso. ($\quad = 112.$)

Piano.

1) (Continue with the Finale, on p. 238.)

№ 18. Epithalamium.[+)]

seul_ est ma vi - e, À lui ma foi, Le sort sans pi - tié l'a sé - pa -
him was all my plea - sure, My life was he, Yet for - tune un - kind holds him a -

sort im - pla - cable Il faut su - bir la loi, Du sort im - pla - cable Il faut su -
fate hath in store, our hearts can ne'er for - see! What fate hath in store, our hearts can

cœur va pour ja - mais_ T'en - ga - ger sa foi, Mon cœur pour ja - mais va t'en - ga -
heart for aye to thine_ shall u - nit - ed be, My heart shall for aye to thine u -

âme a - mou - reu - se Su - bit ta loi, Son cœur pour ja - mais va t'en - ga -
heart owns thy pow - er, And glows for thee, His heart shall for aye to thine u -

à - me a - mou - reu - se Su - bit ta loi, Son cœur pour ja - mais va t'en - ga -
heart owns thy pow - er, And glows for thee, His heart shall for aye to thine u -

Son à _ me su - bit ta loi, Son cœur pour ja - mais va t'en - ga -
His heart on - ly glows for thee! His heart shall for aye to thine u -

cœur va pour ja - mais T'en - ga - ger sa foi, Son cœur pour ja - mais va t'en - ga -
heart for aye to thine shall u - nit - ed be, His heart shall for aye to thine u -

Ton à - me peut croire en moi. Le ciel te pro - tége et veil - le -
Thy heart yet may trust in me, For heav'n shall pro - tect and shall watch

Nº 19. Finale.

fil-le, cède aux vœux du fi-an-cé qui t'ai-me! Le ciel va vous u-
daughter, yield thy heart, love him who doth a - dore thee! E - ter - nal are the

nir par des nœuds é - -ter - nels! De cet hy-men bé - ni____ voi-
ties that your love shall in - vest. Now is the hour su - preme____ of

ci l'in-stant su - prê - me! Le bonheur vous at - tend au__ pied des
wedded life be - fore__ thee! Sweet the joys that a - wait thee at__ yon

saints au - tels,__ Le bon-heur vous at-tend au pied des saints au-
al - tar blest, sweet the joys that a - wait thee at__ yon al- -tar

Moderato.

tels!__
blest!__

cresc. molto.

Act V.

№ 20. Entr'acte.

№ 20ᵇⁱˢ. Scene.

The Tomb.

№ 21. Juliet's Slumber.

№ 22. Scene and Duet.

C'est là! ———
'Tis here! ———

Andante.   (with an expression of awe.)

Sa - lut! __   tom-
Oh tomb! __   Thy

beau!   sombre et si - len - ci - eux! __   Un tom-
frown   dark - ly my gaze de - fies! __   A

beau!   non   non! __   ô   de-meu-re plus bel - le
tomb!   No,   no! __   Oh   yet love-lier a   dwell - ing

Que le sé-jour mê - me des   cieux! _____   Sa - lut, __ pa - lais __ splen-
Than yon fair a - bode in the   skies! _____   How bright   thy   front! A

Recit.

dide et ra - di - eux! __   Ah! la voi - là! c'est el -
pal - ace it out - vies! __   Ah, she is there, my dar-

core, Et sou-rire à l'é-ter-ni-té!!!
per-ish, Like a smile on e-ter-ni-ty!

Pourquoi me la rends-tu si belle, ô mort li-
Why give her me a-gain so love-ly, thou pale de-

vi-de?... Est-ce pour me je-ter plus vi-te dans ses bras?
stroy-er? Is it to draw me ear-lier yet to her em-brace?

Va! c'est le seul bon-heur dont mon cœur soit a-vi-de!... Et ta proie aujourd'-
Ah! it is on-ly thus that my heart can en-joy her! And thy prey shall to-

hui ne t'é-chap-pe-ra pas.
night here meet thee face to face!

Andante. (♩ = 66.)

Ah!_ je te con-tem-ple sans crainte, Tombe où je vais en-fin_ près
Ah!_ Less have I dread-ed thee nev-er, Tomb where I shall at last_ re-

d'el - le re - po - ser!_ Ô mes bras,_ don-nez-
pose, no more to grieve; Oh my arms!_ This em-

lui vo - tre dernière é - trein-te! Mes lè-vres, don-nez-lui vo-tre der-
brace shall be your last for ev - er! My lips,_ take ye now a long fare-

Andante.

(he embraces Juliet deliriously.)

nier _ bai - ser!... _
well _ to love! _

ff (with frenzy.)   (He empties the vial at one

À toi, ma Ju-li - et - te!
To thee, O, my be-lov- ed!

draught, and casts it on the ground; then reels, and sinks gradually on the steps of the monument. At

this moment, Juliet begins to shake off her lethargy; she rises slowly, and gazes about her with a be-

wildered air.)

Juliet.

Où suis - je?
Where am I?

Romeo. (listening.)

Ô ver-
Oh a-

ti - ge!
maze - ment!

Est- ce un rê - ve?
Am I dream - ing?

Sa bouche a mur- mu- ré
'Twas sure-ly she who spoke!

mes doigts en fré- mis-
My hands, touch-ing her

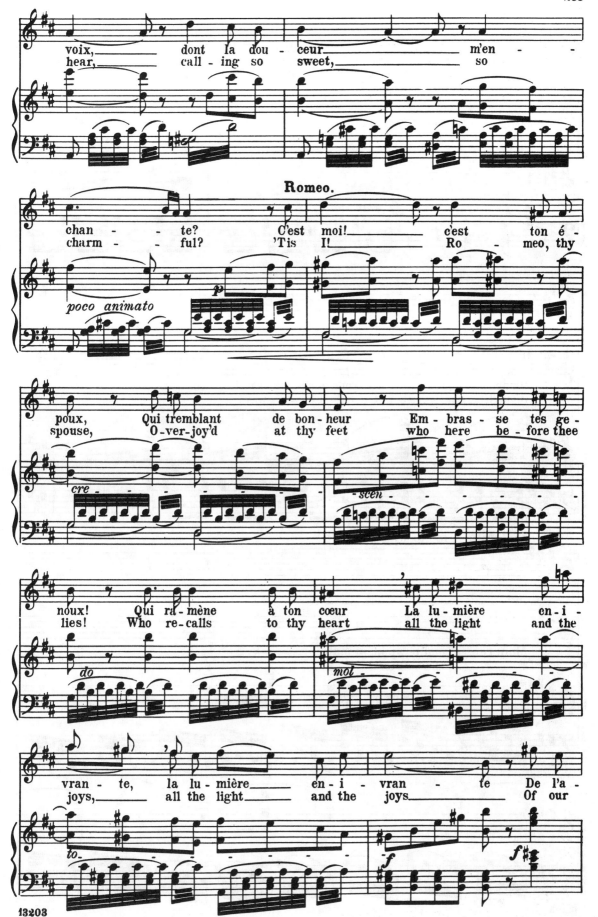

voix,_____ dont la dou - ceur_____ m'en -
hear,_____ call - ing so sweet,_____ so

Romeo.

poco animato

chan - te? C'est moi!_____ c'est ton é -
charm - ful? 'Tis I!_____ Ro - meo, thy

poux, Qui tremblant de bon - heur Em - bras - se tes ge -
spouse, O - ver - joy'd at thy feet who here be - fore thee

cre - - - - - - - - scen - - - - -

noux! Qui ra - mène à ton cœur La lu - mière en - i -
lies! Who re - calls to thy heart all the light and the

do - - - - - - - - mol - - - - -

vran - te, la lu - mière_____ en - i - vran - te De l'a -
joys,_____ all the light_____ and the joys_____ Of our

to - - - - - - - - - f - - - - f

Allegro molto.

Juliet.

(despairingly.)

les pa - rents ont tous des en - trail - les de pier - re! Que dis-
Why are all, ay, all of our kin ston-y-heart - ed? Why is

Allegro molto.

Romeo.

tu?... Ro - mé - o! _____ Ni lar - mes, ni pri-
this? Ro - meo! _____ Nor weep - ing, nor en-

è - re, Rien, ___ rien ne peut les at - ten - drir! _____
treat - ies, Naught, ___ naught can move them to com - ply! _____

À la por - te des cieux, Ju - li-
At the por - tal of heav'n, my be-

et - te, à la por - te des cieux! _____
lov - ed, at the por - tal of heav'n! _____

C'est le doux ros-si-gnol,— con-fi-dent de l'a-
'Tis the sweet night-in-gale,— that of love sings a

pp

Allegro. (♩ = 66.)   Juliet.

mour!— Ah!—
lay!— Ah!—

p   *cresc.*   *molto*   *ff*

_ cru-el é-poux!_ de se poi-son fu-
_ thou cru-el man!_ Why hast thou so be-

ff

nes-te Tu ne m'as pas lais-sé ma part!—
reft me? There is no poi-son here for me!—

f   *dim.*   *ff*

a tempo

allarg.   Ah!— for-tu-né poi-gnard!—
Ah!— yet a way I see!—
a tempo

ff

End of Opera.